LETTERS FROM THE GREAT BLASKET

Letters from
the Great Blasket

by

EIBHLÍS NÍ SHÚILLEABHÁIN

THE MERCIER PRESS
DUBLIN AND CORK

THE MERCIER PRESS,
4 Bridge Street, Cork.
25 Lower Abbey Street, Dublin.

©   Niamh Bean Uí Laoithe

ISBN O 85342 526 4

First edition 1978
Reprinted 1979

Printed by Litho Press Co., Midleton, Co. Cork.

CONTENTS

INTRODUCTION

In 1931, George Chambers of 64, Temple Fortune Lane, London NW 11, visited the Great Blasket island off the Kerry coast and made the acquaintance of Eibhlís Ní Shúilleabháin, a native of the Irish-speaking island, who was then a girl of twenty. So began a correspondence that was to last for some thirty years, and was not interrupted even by the most significant event in the life of Eibhlís, her departure with her husband and daughter from the Great Blasket on 14 July, 1942. Chambers preserved the letters which he received from Eibhlís and her immediate family and later prepared them for publication. In the introduction to this work (never actually published), which he proposed to call *The Letters of Eibhlís,* he describes his first visit to the island and gives his impressions of the place:-

> In the summer of 1931 I intended visiting the lighthouse on the lonely and remote Tiaracht Rock that lies out in the Atlantic beyond County Kerry and is the most westerly point of Europe. It is not easy to get on the Rock and I was advised to make the island of Blasket my headquarters and get the fisherfolk to take me out to the lighthouse. This was the first time that I had heard of Blasket, so, finding 'school' marked on Bartholomew's map, I wrote to the schoolmaster for help in getting lodgings etc. The reply came from Nora O'Shea, the mistress, who fixed me up

for lodgings and arranged for a boat to meet me when I arrived.

The railway proper ends at Tralee and from that town a very primitive railway goes right over the top of a range of mountains — with lovely vistas of sea and mountain on either side — down to the fairly large town of Dingle. From there I had to take a motor, by way of Ventry and Slea Head along one of the famous 'Famine Roads', to Dunquin, a bleak, impoverished and scattered village lying under a bare mountain side. The cliffs here are some two hundred feet high and, about three miles out in the Atlantic, was the huge but narrow bulk of Blasket, rising to nearly a thousand feet but nowhere more than half-a-mile wide; around it were some five or six attendant islands, none of them inhabited, and three miles further out in the ocean could be seen the sharp pyramid of the Tiaracht Rock.

On the evening of my arrival at Dunquin the sea was too stormy for a boat to put out so I stayed the night at the post-office where the red-headed and unmarried post-mistress made me welcome and treated me remarkably well, everything being very clean and the food good. The next morning — Saturday — my boat, or rather canvas canoe for there is no other kind of craft on Blasket, came across for me. These canoes are made of tarred canvas stretched over a framework of open lattice, are about eighteen feet long, and there are usually four rowers, each pulling two almost bladeless oars; three passengers, all sitting in the bottom of the boat, make a full load.

There is only one landing-place on the island for canoes, a tiny harbour that has been made by joining a great rock to the shore by a concrete barrier. From this slipway a steep path runs up to the top of cliff and into the village. Every house, or rather cabin, on Blasket is in this little village which lies irregularly up the side of the hill. They are all, with the exception of five, the usual Irish type, built of rough stones with little evidence of mortar, they have one fairly large general room and one or two smaller rooms. There is only the one front door, no house has a back entrance. They are all roofed with tarred felt or canvas and most of them have a small loft over the fireplace.

The five exceptions were built by the Congested Districts Board, these are concrete and have slate roofs and are all placed in un-picturesque and exposed positions and al-though a benevolent government gave them back-doors they omitted to explain what their use might be, so the islanders have nailed them up and now use them for dressers. All of the cabins have earth floors, and as all

9

the poultry and animals — including cats, dogs, sheep and donkeys — have the run of the cabins it is the duty of one of the children of the house to be continually scattering fresh sand on the floor . . .

To a person who has not had the actual experience, or merely visited the island on a warm summer's day, it is difficult to make it clear what is meant by the bald statements that there is no shop on the island, no doctor, no nurse, no priest, no church and no landlord. Many of the children have never seen a tree or anything that goes on wheels, while gas and electric light are unknown mysteries.

On the afternoon of my first day I was strolling up the hillside when I met two girls coming down with their ass who was loaded with two panniers of turf. Both the girls were bareheaded and wore neither shoes nor stockings and were clothed in little more than rags, but two more beautiful girls I have seldom seen and they were as merry and unaffected with me as though I had been an elder brother; this was my first meeting with Eibhlís and her sister Mary.

The Eibhlís mentioned above is Eibhlís Ní Shúilleabháin, the author of almost all the letters, a selection of which is now published here for the first time. Chambers visited the Great Blasket and Eibhlís for the second and final time in the summer of 1938. By now Eibhlís had married Seán Ó Criomhthain (generally referred to in the letters as John [Crohan], a son of Tomás Ó Criomhthain, *An tOileánach (The Islandman)*. In fact Eibhlís was already closely related to Tomás, her grandmother, Máire, being his sister; hence she refers to him as her granduncle before her marriage to Seán, and as her father-in-law subsequently. On her marriage she lived in the same house as the Islandman and nursed him during the last years of his life which are described in the letters. Incidentally, the collection includes what must be an almost unique specimen of the Islandman's writing in English, in the form of a letter expressing his good-will towards Chambers. Apart from this, and a few written by her husband Seán, all the letters published here were written by Eibhlís herself.

The original manuscripts of the letters for the period covered here have not been preserved, or at least were not available to the present editor. However, it is clear from an examination of his trans-scriptions of some later letters that Chambers was scrupulously exact with regard to such matters as spelling, punctuation, grammar and syntax, and only very minor changes, and these in the interests of intellegibility, were thought desirable here. A few Irish words which Chambers obviously didn't under-stand have been restored to their proper form. Similarly the initial arrangement of the subject matter has been generally followed: the material is arranged under various headings in chronological order, the different sections running concurrently. The most substantial change is in the amount of

11

material utilised; due to considerations of space this has been reduced to perhaps a third of its original length. Further to this the present edition concentrates on those passages which describe various aspects of life on the Great Blasket prior to the departure of Eibhlís. The island was to remain inhabited for a further eleven years but it is already clear by 1942 what the ending must be.

Love of the Great Blasket, its people and its ways, and the fear of what it holds for herself and her family, and particularly for her infant daughter, Niamh, are the conflicting emotions about which the letters are constructed. The conflict was partially resolved by the removal of the little family to the mainland of Muiríoch where Eibhlís spent the remainder of her life but, as is clear from subsequent letters, the focal point of her existence still remained the Great Blasket which she could now visit only occasionally in summer. Though still living in an Irish-speaking area, only about 10 miles from her island home, her exile was almost as complete as the more usual one endured by the many other islanders of her generation who had long since departed for the United States.

Here in the letters, through the struggling idiom and laboured passages, emerges the fascinating detail of a strange and different way of life as seen unconsciously through the eyes of a woman, seen from the inside. Here the struggle is not for the luxury of meaning in existence, but for existence itself, and while the result may not be high literature it is nevertheless compelling reading.

Seán Ó Coileáin

I

The Old Home

8.9.31. You would not like to stay here during the winter I am sure. It is a dull place in winter, nothing atall only the pleasant music of the wild seas and the clattering of the wind, but for all I like it anyway, because my dear there is no place like home. My cottage home at the foot of the mountain, and the very day I'll have to leave it won't be a pleasant day for me. I think my dear heart will break that day. Would you guess that? I was born Saturday, 6 May, 1911, and I suppose that will be twenty-one next May. I am very old indeed I don't feel so atall. I have no sense yet.

I work at home and get the necessary things of life from father. I work at the turf, of course you saw some of that yourself. We are digging the potatoes now. I do pick them and bring them home on the donkey. I also sew and knit for father and brothers. But for money I don't see it atall unless going to town for anything.

All the old women, nearly, spin but there is no weaving here, I mean on the Island. Did you ever see my mother spinning? I thought you did. My mother's name is Johanna Dunleavy.

Did I ever tell you anything about my two other

brothers. Yes I think I didn't. Pádraig is my eldest brother and Mike is my second brother. Mary the third, myself the fourth and Seán the youngest. Five in family and we are all nearly big now and we are altogether yet. Thank God. I often hear people saying that the best part of life is when the family are together. I would believe it too unless they would be very poor altogether.

9.11.31. From the 1st November we have an awful bad weather here, wind and rain nearly every day. Very dark evenings and fine long nights. I don't feel the bad nights at present anyway, reading *The Crock of Gold* around the fire. It is very nice and funny, and also the dictionary with me all the time. One paraffin lamp in the kitchen that's all. We use candles in our room. We sometimes have a look at *The Kerryman* and *Irish Press*. Nora [Nora O'Shea, the schoolmistress] gets them papers twice weekly, she passes them around of course. I don't work much, winter now, I don't even go to the hill but to the strand for sand with the donkey, some evenings sewing and knitting sometimes reading.

12.1.32. Today morning was very fine. I thought that the postman would go across anyway. Everyone on the Blasket got themselves ready for the hill. Some brought their asses to bring turf, others brought their cows and calves, while yet others went strolling looking for sheep. They were not an hour gone when it began to rain terrible. Nobody expected it so soon. They are home now drenched. The turf and the people and animals are all wet. Dad and Pádraig

14

are putting on their new clothes after the morning. The cows are driven home now, everything locked up in its own place after the rain and storm. I think no one will stir tonight. Reading will be delightful tonight. Does any bad day or night like this come in London?

It was too cold and we gathered around the fire. Daddy was singing old songs for us. He can sing very well and the old Irish songs that are not written in books atall at present are very nice to hear. After the Rosary we went to bed. I slept sound until morning. When I opened the door it was not so grand a view I got. I first set my eyes on the sea, but alas no hope either today of any boat crossing. If it was fine and sunny on the land itself here we don't call it fine until the sea is calm.

After awhile I drove up my cow and calf, because they were inside yesterday.

14.3.32. Of our family indeed it is hard to tell what is before us in this life. You know in the passed years as they were grown up here they used go to America one after one. The eldest first and then every year from that out one after one would go through her until the last of the family. No one is going at present but we all hope for better life yet.

I suppose Mary would be thinking of going to America. Seán is thinking of joining the Civic Guard in a couple of years time. There are lots of boys from here in them you know. Pádraig my eldest brother may yet marry here, and Mike and myself I don't know what will become of us. We must go through life of course and we won't get it atall as we like to. Oh I know. Inside in my heart I love to stay at home if I'd have any work to do to live on like having a nice house and having lodgers in summer here. I would love that but I don't know will that ever come true. I have no thoughts of getting married atall yet.

22.3.32. I was on the hill today morning with my cow and calf and donkey. I left them with the cows and went for a load of turf, old turf. Everyone in the house except Mother and Mary, were in the strand for weed — you know sea-weed for manuring — and most of the Islanders too were there. When the tide is very very low they go out on the stones or rocks and cut if off with knives and then put it together in a rope and put it on their backs then. They bring it to the fields that's near on their backs but the donkeys bring it if the fields are too far off. They do be very wet and they are all changing their clothes now after coming home.

16.7.32. I am not on the hill atall today, I am cleaning up my room here, whitewashing it first. It's easy to do so because it is a small room and there is nothing in it but a table, a cupboard and our bed. Also a chair. There walls are decorated with postcards from you. There are no fine pictures on the walls atall. I am here sitting on my bed now writing you this and you are in some fine house or hotel in the island at Donegal.

3.8.32. There isn't so much people in any house in the Island. In our house imagine Father and

An island woman spinning.

Mother in bed, Pádraig and Mike in a bed, Seán and my grandfather in a bed, and Mary and myself in another bed, two beds in one room and one bed in the other two rooms. Three rooms we have. I am very sure that in some of the houses — small houses you know where — there isn't but one room with two beds in it. Some of them sleep in the loft of the room in a checker down you see. Small children, two and three, can sleep in one room. I often saw, when we were small ourselves, I do think of Mary and myself sleeping in the bed with Father and Mother, two in the head of the bed (we say in Irish *i gceann*) and the other two below *(i gcos)*. When we were bigger Daddy built a small cosy room for us and we are there since.

II

Marriage and Childbirth

12.5.33. Well friend I am at home at present with my future husband John Crohan, Tomás Crohan's son. I was married with John last Saturday (May the sixth), my twenty-second birthday the day before it, ın Ballyferriter by Rev N. Brown, P.P. We had only two motorcars. We came from town there and then off again to Dingle Town after Mass, few Islanders attended because of the weather being far from fine. I was in my little Island home then again at about nine o'clock Saturday night, I mean in my new house, but not yet the house of my dreams but some day yet with God's help. Well friend just another few words on this subject, I love my husband and my home, all the world has changed to me, everything for the better. Let us all praise God in Heaven.

All my friends here gave me every help for my wedding only for them I would have a great trouble to make up the deficit. So it was very hard as every thing in town is as expensive as it could be, but now thank God it's over.

12.6.33. Well good friend, the details of the wedding are few, but anyway I'll make my best to tell you. Mary and myself went out Tuesday before. We walked it from Dunquin into town (about twelve miles). We rested in town for a few days and then we brought everything necessary for the wedding day, which was Saturday after, such as a blue dress with white collar and cuffs, a long one too, a pair of black shoes, and a new shawl and we dressed the same though Mary was not my bridesmaid for John's niece came from Burnham College Dingle that morning — named Mary Malone — and she was the one, then Pádraig was John's best man.

Friday evening John (my husband), Pádraig, Seán and my uncle came to town. My husband John came in to see me that evening and showed me the ring and told me to wear it so that he could see would it suit my finger. Well I tried it on and it fitted all right so he took it away again until tomorrow morning.

They stayed in another house in town and early Saturday morning a motor stopped at Mrs Curran's house and someone was knocking at the door. We were ready and we went out, there were two motors there, I did not go in with John atall, because it is said here around in every place that it is unlucky to go with him in the motorcar to the church. Is it like that in London?

At eight o'clock the ring was fitted rightly on my finger and Eibhlís of the Island was Mrs Eibhlís of the Island and everything was changed for the better thank God.

We went to town again and had breakfast in Keane's house and done lots of messages there again. We had some dancing there too and Seán was playing the violin and we all enjoyed the evening until rather late. Then we got all parcels and luggage packed and we had then a good drive to Dunquin.

The night was lovely, there wasn't a stir in the air and the sea was like glass. The moon was just coming up and now and then a black cloud which was passing would darken the world but when that would pass it, the moon would come out again and was surely looking down on a small canoe with four men rowing and two women seated in its end. The man next to the younger of the two men was the husband, next to him was the bride, so calm and lovely with her dark brown eyes admiring the loveliness of the world.

So now dear friend I am a very very happy bride with a dear husband and home in this Island.

23.2.36. Yes, I am the only girl that got married since you were here and I am married three years next May 6th and it was twelve years before that since the last couple were married. Anyway at present nobody thinks of marrying. I suppose it's the bad weather that's coming with the last forty years down that's getting on their nerves. The girls here would marry in the morning but the boys don't agree with that. They know well that it is not any joke to be married on an Island like this and to bring up families like their fathers did and then not to have enough to eat nor to give them any chance atall in life afterwards.

19.1.37. The terrible time [of childbirth] is coming near so in three or four weeks time I shall be

21

preparing to go out. You know I am going to a friend's house near Dingle, Nurse Kate Malone's house. They have seven children there but the wife have asked me to come to them as the weather may be rough and terrible by the time I would want it fine and that it would be safer for me to be near the town then.

18.3.37. Well dearest, my husband was here from Sunday until today with me, and as there was no owner at home he had to go in [to the Island] again today, and I never felt so lonely since I came here as I do tonight and all day since he went.

I hope to God I will be all right myself in a little time. I am here five weeks yesterday, what a change since and what a long time from home, but God is good and I trust in Him that all will be well with us very soon.

1.5.37. Thanks be to God I am over my trouble and able to write to you again and to do all my work. I am a happy mother since with a lovely baby daughter Niamh it was about time for me to get that happiness too.

I am ready to leave this place tomorrow as my husband promised to come and bring me home, the weather is awful fine. He is a very proud Daddy mind you.

28.5.37. Well dearest I suppose you know I have been very much taken up since Niamh was born but I am so delighted with her that I like to be always with her. I am afraid I have been neglecting my husband John since she came and all my friends especially you . . . . A cradle in a corner of the house is very strange of course here and strange to all Islanders.

(a) The Islandman

3.8.32. Well Tomás Ó Criomhthain or in English Thomas Crohan is my granduncle. Don't be surprised at that, and I am very fond of him. He won a statue of Queen Taillean and a very nice gold and silver medal – from Dublin they both came. His book was the very best book ever written in Irish or English too I am very sure you'll read it but I don't know will I because it will be dearer – now 7/6 – I think but of course it will be worth it. I read it once in Irish because he has one at home himself but I don't know will there be any chance of this. You know he does be at us for not buying it in Irish but once in a year or two we go to town we don't ever remember buying it. It was 3/6 in Irish namely *An tOileánach* it must be in English *The Islandman.*

You know he is talking of my grandfather and grandmother and all the old plants and also, all about himself and his family and how they all went away from him, died you know. They are all dead only his two sons, one here, his name is John, he is an unmarried man, I think he is twenty-nine years are so, the other is in America and he is married, Tomás is his name. Poor Uncle he had a big family once and they were the loveliest family here, so may they all rest in peace Amen. He also talks about himself in the book and how he was in love with a very nice girl once, I think she was living in Inishvickillane, you know that island where we had tea the day we were in Tiaracht.

That's the time you'll know everything about the Island long ago when you'll read *The Islandman*.

27.4.33. I heard that Mr Flower had fallen from a horse and that his head was injured. Only half of my granduncle's book is translated by him yet.

17.10.33. [Eibhlís has now married John.] Well my father-in-law made little money of his book. Robin Flower have promised to have it ready (I mean published in English) in November then I hope you'll have it read before Christmas, so you'll know all about him then and you'll understand everything. Mr Flower ought to have it translated long ago he would have it ready but he was sick.

17.10.33. [A letter from John.] According to our book, it was not very successful Irish books do not bring much money for Readers are scarce as you ought to know that. The manuscript was given to the Government for £60 and that was all the money my father got for it. There is an English translation in two month's time and it is a wonder that you do not know that from Robin Flower. Who have done so. The next time you will call to the Museum you can have some talk with Him about it. I guess it is nearly Finished by Him.

You know it should be Published long ago by Jonathan Cape But it took too Long and He gave it up so now it will be published By the Educational Co. of Ireland, Dublin.

It was a great Loss for us for O'Sullivan's book *Twenty Years A-Growing* took the market from us and that is the Reason Cape gave it up. Flower should have the translation done within nine months but he was sick and could not Have the work done in time. So it can't Be Helped and We do not Blame any Body.

My father is moving on yet.

So Long and Good Luck to you all. J. Crohan.

2.11.33. Everyone on the Island are well and happy thank the Lord, except my father-in-law, he does be sick oftener in winter time. He does be very cold.

7.12.33. If you could come here in an airoplane you could sit down by a nice cosy fire here with my father-in-law. How would I like to be listening to you both talking English. I couldn't so very well speak it. I would do something in writing.

10.1.34. Father-in-law feels terrible cold some days and does not get up atall. He is getting old too now. Is it not a pity, poor father-in-law.

[A letter from the 'Islandman.'] I want to let you know that I Like you very much. I think it is the only way for doing so is to drop you few lines But to tell the truth It comes very Difficult on me to write in English for to tell the truth as you know what I am writing I hardly understand it. But if you know Irish Language I tell you That you would get it.

I hope you are enjoying life the same as you want

to do so that's what some people would say. But that
is not the way may be. But I hope not.

We do feel tired these days after working from 7
in the morning to 6 in the evening.

The young lads here have an English phrase since
you left, you used to say 'Fine morning' and They
have the same since.

Good Bye now and a Happy Long Life. T. Crohan.

3.5.34. [A letter from John.] My father's book
The Islandman is going to be published in a month's
time or so. When it will come out you need not buy
a copy for I will ask my father to present you with a
Copy a thing that He is willing to do. The old man is
getting weak every day now and I suppose he won't
do no more writing. John Crohan.

10.9.34. Many thanks for the information about
The Islandman. My father-in-law is very grateful to
you because he didn't hear with a very long time
anything about the book.

1.11.34. With your letter yesterday came half a
dozen of the books *The Islandman* from Chatto and
Windus. What a pity you have bought a one, I am
sorry you have done so, because I will send you a
copy with joy, but how late they came anyhow. I
hope you'll like it well and will think lots of my
father-in-law after reading it.

12.11.34. I am glad you have read the book and
has enjoyed it so much. Well the word 'Kitchen'
means: When the potatoes are put on the table here,
and if you were to eat them without meat or fish or
anything, we would say we hadn't any kitchen with

the potatoes today. Here in Irish it is called whatever
things you would eat with the potatoes, whether it is
fish or meat. I think it is oftener called sauce. Also
when drinking tea and bread you call the butter and
eggs the kitchen with tea. My grandmother mentioned in *The Islandman* is Tomás's sister Máire, the
widow who left them the child and went to America.
After her returning home she married my grandfather,
you saw him in my house at home, you offered him
cigarettes that day do you remember?

29.12.35. My father-in-law is a little better, he gets
up every day and I hope he will be lots better when
summer comes.

22.1.36. I am very sorry to say or to have to
tell you of the terrible week we had last week. My
father-in-law got a terrible pain in his legs and in all
his bones, we thought he was dead in the middle of
the night, next day he was anointed. Two priests
came to him, one of them a visitor staying in Dunquin and the day was lovely. After the priest he got
a relief from the pains but we stayed up with him
three long nights and they were as cold as anything.
I never before felt the cold so bad, because I wasn't
accustomed to staying up atall. It's a terrible thing
in winter I tell you. But thank God for it, a couple
of nights were not atall bad and he is a little better
again at present. It must be rheumatic pains he had,
getting up didn't suit him atall. He is in bed with a
fortnight now without any intention of getting up.
He never got any pain before in all his life. Anyway
he is old but I don't know how would we manage

Taking produce to the mainland in a currach.

without him and I hope God he will live until long
and fine summer days will come. That's the worst
about Islands to have old people here in winter.

26.1.36. My father-in-law did not get up yet, of
course the weather is too bad, but when the weather
will clear up a bit maybe with great care he may
come to the fire poor man. So that's the way.

7.7.36. My father-in-law is very crippled at
present, hardly he gets up atall now, and I have to
take great care about him (now in bed you know)
and all the visitors come to see him still, but I like
to do whatever I can for the poor man. It's terrible
to be so old.

5.11.36. We had great fun the evening the parcel
came. John brought it in, there was a middle-aged
man from the Island inside, so we put the parcel on
the table and opened it out. He was much surprised
of all in it and he at once thought of giving my
father-in-law the boots and hat and white shirt in it,
so I brought them down to him and as you know
yourself, he is just like a child now, there was nothing
troubling him when he handled them but the fear of
them being taken away again from him and wasn't it
a good thing to put them above his bed so that he
can always be eyeing them. He was told that it was
'Chambers' that had sent them to him, ah he remembers 'Chambers' always. The hat was put on his head
inside in bed and it suited him lovely because it is
small; so said that man inside that he didn't laugh as
much with a long time.

Seldom he gets up now, but a few nights ago he

got up, John put the hat on him and told him it was like his own hat, you know the big black rimmed hat he used wear, and when the small one was on his head, he said that 'Chambers' hat brings more light to his eyes. We have great fun on him when he is up like that, although he speaks very very little he is strong but he hasn't any memory.

17.12.36. Yes, my father-in-law is a great trouble to us with a year and a half now. I think his right age is seventy-nine now, but all the same poor man, he was all right when there wasn't much more to do in the house but if there were as I hope God there soon will be indeed, he must be forgotten oftener, but God is good and puts everything in order in good time.

19.1.37. [Eibhlís's time is near and she is to go to Dingle.] I do hate thinking of leaving my home for my father-in-law is so helpless and I am so used to him now I think anyone else would not understand him so well. So God is good and everything will come all right, I hope and trust in Him.

9.3.37. [Written from Dingle.] I am here a month tomorrow March 10th, and I didn't see anyone from home until Sunday at eleven o'clock. My husband John came and my brother Pádraig and oh Mr Chambers, they just stayed ten minutes with me for they were in a great hurry for I must tell and write it down for you in deepest regret that my dearest father-in-law died peacefully and passed away to his reward at seven o'clock that Sunday morning, oh may he rest in peace, Amen, and how I missed being from my home and from his funeral yesterday God only knows. You know they would not leave me travelling to Dunquin as I am so near the time now and I hope God that good news will come to me and that I will be all right soon again for to go home and look after my dear husband. I feel how my husband felt last night, after the funeral and no one to comfort him at home but God did so I hope and His Holy Mother.

So now, dear friend, how quickly death steals our friends and dear ones and you know how I feel out here and my poor father-in-law buried yesterday. It was God's will to take him away, and may His will always be done and not ours.

18.3.37. When everything will be settled again, with God's help I will tell you more of my father-in-law and what did he mean to us, but as he was so helpless my husband and I are glad and thankful to God who called him to Himself, for he was suffering and we did hate to see him like that. May God rest his soul.

6.5.40. Tomás' mother, Seán tells me was about forty-five when he — Tomás — was born. Lord have mercy on the dead.

(b) Peig

3.2.40. Peig Sayers is a little bit well off than the beginning of her life as she told you herself. She got money through her son's death in America, maybe a few hundreds, the most beautiful boy you ever saw, she well paid for them. Who would envy her of that money when it broke her heart first? Then she got it out of books, her second story-book is selling at present, did I tell you that? It is very nice and interesting . . .

Then Peig is getting old now and she is always weather-bound since she came to the Island, living in a lonely cottage now on with only her one son and he getting on in years with no wife or family or nothing of life's joy which no money would buy but which you could not have without money, no cow or milk to spare, I may say not much to comfort them atall. If she was somewhere near town or near a chapel Peig would walk out and refresh herself with something — anyway she would be quite happy to go to Mass Sundays, or evenings a gay talk with someone, or see cars and people of the world passing her. She has nothing to make her happy here, no hope atall.

6.11.42. You may have heard that also our Queen Peig has come out [from the island] and is once more living in Dunquin in her native place; her brother-in-law was very very lonely but Mike [her son] was not, nor either Peig I heard. So pity our Island without either King or Queen this winter nor children on its ground, no wonder it's lonely and sad after all the gay families and all its children in foreign grounds. Remember [when] you once told me that Peig – the Queen – must be very happy there on the Island, I told you there was nothing there in life to make her happy and like all Queens she had a bit of money too but far from being happy, nobody knows the worries and nervous that follows an Islander's life.

28.3.48. Peig is an invalid – at present home with her son the Poet – and does not leave her bed since suffering from a nasty fall near her home some time last year. Someone told me she was nearly blind now and hasn't so well a time there as no woman around the house. Poor Peig, our Past Queen, was very very nice indeed and a lovely company. So that is the way with life; people suffer a lot all the life. I wish Peig had a more comfortable home now in the end of her days.

12.7.48. Poor Peig Sayers is still an invalid in her bed near the fire and the old brother-in-law in the house died lately, only herself and the poet now remains, but she is far from being the Queen now as they isn't many servants to wait on her the poor woman. It's bad to be without a daughter or daughter-in-law in the end.

9.1.49. The Queen of the Island Peig Sayers is

still living but she do not leave her bed atall the poor woman. I hear she is getting blind too God help us. It's sad to be old and have no one I mean any wife or girl to take care of you.

IV

Death on the Island

9.11.31. When there is a dead man on Blaskets everybody is frightened, anyway the children and nearly grownups also. A boat with four men of crew goes out to Dunquin immediately after his departure from this life. They go to town in a car from Dunquin. There are also a woman in the car. They always have the woman from Dunquin. It is superstitious to have her with them atall you know. They bring the coffin and everything necessary for the wake in this car, things such as pipes, tobacco, white bread, teas, jam and they arrive in Blaskets as soon as possible — the very same night. If bad weather they stay until the morrow.

If he is an old man, it will be a funny night of course. Another man will be telling stories, fairy tales and young people will be throwing bits of clay pipes on one another and them sort of sport. But of course when there is a young person there are no fun atall.

When persons come in the first time to see the dead, he will kneel at his side and say a prayer with his poor soul. Then the following day he will be buried. When he is put into the coffin and taken on the shoulders of four men, there is a boreen here and

35

we call it the 'Boreen of the Dead', and wherever place the coffin is taken out of it will come all the way and down through this road or boreen. All the canoes here go in the funeral and the canoe with the coffin will be the first and the rest after it then. Also women and young girls go, one in every canoe nearly, sometimes. Some of the people are buried in Dunquin others in Ventry.

7.1.32. I was on a wake since. Here an old man died unexpected last Sunday. He went to bed Saturday night good enough and was dying in the morning. He was dead altogether then about four o'clock Sunday evening. He was Pats Kearney's father-in-law. He was seventy years of age. He lived with his sister in one of the cottages, the new ones. Then Sunday evening they went out for the coffin and wake. Pats Kearney and two other men. They went to town that night and brought the coffin in a motor car or lorry I think, to Dunquin. It was too late then to come in that night. It was also rather bad so they came in Monday evening and indeed it was not fine at sea atall. The dead body was inside Monday night also as it was too bad and too late.

All the Islanders were gathered in the house the two nights. I was there myself the first night. The body was laid out on the bed and was very nice to look on. On the floor of the room we were sitting (all the girls and a couple of old women). It was a funny night to us. Telling stories and everything to shorten the night . . At twelve o'clock we all kneeled down in the room and also the people in the kitchen and we said the Rosary. It was delightful. We had tea then about two o'clock. Tea and bread and jam. It wasn't so plentiful you know because as the wake didn't come that night. We were there until eight in the morning and then we went home. We did not go to sleep atall but I was not there the second night but to twelve o'clock. It went on as the night before. He was put into the coffin then at twelve noon the next day. Then the old women cried on him. That is a custom here. Tuesday evening he was buried. When the coffin was taken out all things that's used about the corps [corpse] are also taken outside the house. Four chairs are under the coffin then and they cried again. The coffin was taken down to the canoe on the shoulders of four men.

The day was very bad and only two boats went out. The one with the corps [corpse] and another one. They came home yesterday evening. Also a child died, three months old. He was buried the same day in our Temple. [Unconsecrated ground.] Did you ever see it? Small children are buried there. His father was with us to the Tiaracht. He is Pats Kearney's brother. He has nine children yet.

A neighbour has just come in. I hear him saying that another old friend (an old man) or old neighbour of us will soon be dead again. He is very bad unless he'll get anyway better again. I hope he will because I'll tell you. Since the Shea man died we are afraid to stir any night unless three or four of us together. We believe in fairies here; that's why we are so interested in fairy tales. If you were to see the children when there is someone dead here, honestly, they nearly die themselves when they see him. Everyone is frightened until he is buried a month or so. Jerry Shea was from the top of the village but this man is nearer to us down here so I hope he won't die so soon. Do you be afraid of fairies yourself?

1.2.32. Yes, that was the Temple I meant because grown-ups are there too you see. Years ago when people used die in bad weather here they were buried there. I don't remember anyone buried there lately. My grandmother died five or six years ago. It was Christmas time and the weather was fiercefully bad. What was done I'll tell you. They made the coffin themselves, after a few days, and then she was put into it for another day or two and was left in her room until a fine day came. She was taken out then and buried in Dunquin.

People don't die so often here you know as other places and thank the Lord nowadays they get the chance of burying always.

5.3.32. I was on a wake here. John Dunleavy, the man that was sick a spell died early yesterday morning. May his soul R.I.P. Amen. The day was as fine as it could be. His eldest son and wife and two more boys went out early for the wake. If the day wasn't fine enough for a woman from the Island to go out one from Dunquin would go with them to town. I don't understand why the women have to go.

They had a motor car to town, only two of them went there and the two boys went to Ballyferriter to tell the Parish Priest to be in the funeral tomorrow, that is today. The son and his wife in town hired a motor lorry that brought the coffin and other parcels and bags too, including two bags of white bread and a good amount of jam, a box of clay pipes and a few bottles of whiskey, also a half barrel of porter. The wake was here at half-past six yesterday evening and when the coffin comes, the old women do cry. In Irish we call that cry *olagón*. The dead body was laid on his bed with his own new suit on him, only his cap and boots as you know yourself and he was very very nice looking. Everyone on the Island came to see him and said a prayer with his poor soul only the small children because they would be afraid of him you see. The old people here say that if you would touch his hand or forehead when dead, that you would never again be anyway afraid of him to see him or anything, and this we all did. I felt his hand, dear me Mr Chambers he was as cold as ice. Two more canoes came in from the mainland, relatives and friends came from far and near. The house was crowded. We stayed there until eight this morning. We spent the night happily. A spell around the fire, a spell below in the corp's [corpse's]room, everyone deeply interested in the shadow of death. To the sick man it brought peace and rest, to his poor wife, it has left her a lonely widow with her only comfort in life, her only son and daughter far far away from her. She wished they were nigh their father's side this hour anyway. But God help us they were too far away from him. You know the married man in the house is her step-son and there is also a brother of him there, a widower. It is not her own house now.

Saturday: The funeral is gone out today. It went at half-past nine though no one expected it to go until twelve or half twelve, but they always depend on the weather here. The storm was beginning early in the morning and they got everything ready as soon as possible. Five canoes went out with the canoe with the coffin, and that canoe is always the first one and the rest after it then in a straight line. There are only three men in it and the coffin. They were just landed outside when the wind blew terrible and none of them came today. Poor people and they don't like to stay outside like that. Pádraig and Mike are outside from us and one or two from nearly every house in the Island. Sixteen canoes with the one with the dead body, is usually the funeral at sea from Blaskets to Dunquin and that is a sight the Islanders don't easily forget afterwards.

10.1.34. Well I don't think the old women have any special words keening over the body. One may say, 'May God rest your soul in Heaven, May God take your soul,' and so on, then to say Our Father or Hail Mary. I never heard any special sayings.

2.4.34. I have a very very bad news for you this time which is that all the Islanders are mourning after our dear postman, John Keane (King) R.I.P. which died suddenly last Tuesday night. A very small pimple came on his neck, back, and he scratched it, it blood-poisoned him in two or three days' time, and so the weather was awful hot, he used get up every day. He was in Dunquin Friday last for the post and it was on him that day and was dead Tuesday night. Oh Mr Chambers we couldn't get over it! He was also John's first cousin. None of us expected his death as it was a very very great blow to us all Islanders. Everyone liked him, oh everyone. Many the parcels and letters – good letters – he brought in to us. May God rest his soul, Amen.

He left a widow with a family of seven, five girls two boys, the eldest a girl of fifteen, the youngest a baby girl of eight months. Wasn't it a pity. And a very good man at sea, he had great courage at sea and very seldom missed a post day out. Never again a better postman we will see. How we missed him today or yesterday Friday when there is no postman. Next week they say, his sister's son will get it until his own son is at age to leave school. He had the priest and doctor the very same evening he died. His father – 'The King' we used call him – died five years ago. What will she do and the small children isn't it very hard on her. She is not a native here atall she came in to him married. He was only forty-nine years.

5.11.36. A woman died in the Island a week ago, last Monday night a midst a terrible weather. The corp [corpse] was in for three nights, the wake came that night and she was buried the fourth day. May God rest her soul, Amen. The Island was in a very bad state as it looked as if a long storm would come, but God is merciful and showed it to us, by calming it down at sea. All the Islanders were up the three

41

nights and they were just thinking of making a coffin themselves and then take the corp [corpse] to Dunquin any time suitable for going. Her husband had a good hope and told them he would wait another night, so the third day was fine enough to go for the wake and next day was beautiful for the funeral . . . I hope it will be long again before we'll have another wake on our dear Island.

V

Mass and Priests

6.3.32. Today, Sunday, on the Island it is a stormy day. No boat went to Mass and we are expecting the priests tomorrow for the Stations you know. Every Easter they come here and serve Mass in the schoolhouse. It is nicely whitewashed and painted by Nora and the girls. Two boats from the Island usually go for the priests. Three men in every boat but they are not the two that goes every year atall, no they go, all the people around the Island go on the term.

17.10.32. We don't, I mean girls, go to Mass every Sunday atall from this out because hardly the men go, and throughout summer we used not to go every second or third Sunday. All the girls couldn't go at one time you see. I was at Mass myself a few Sundays ago and it was awful wind coming in. There was no other girl outside from the Island that Sunday, so I told myself that the next time I would go out it would be very very fine. Then confession, hardly any Islander go to confession except once in a year and that is when the priests do come for Stations; of course young boys and girls when they get in town maybe a Saturday or in Dunquin some Sunday, they would go to confession, but very seldom they have that chance. The Islanders I think are very holy and haven't got much sins to tell. They are very nice and quiet people here Thank God and very very seldom they do quarrel or do anything wrong on one another because they are all relatives to one another. What would you say yourself?

Well the ordinary prayers said here morning and noon are the Creed, Hail Mary, and the Rosary. Well I once heard a prayer to say when the fire is made up at night and everyone gone to bed but I haven't it in English, I may get it, though there is not a habit in saying it atall here. I never heard anything used at spinning or weaving.

7.7.36.   Great change have come on the Island lately, there was a Mission here, preached by two Redemptorist Fathers. They were here for a week. They blessed everyone and every place, and they left written hard rules for the visitors that come here, no mixed bathing allowed. White Strand for women alone to bathe and bask. There is a sign post near this strand and written on it is 'Women'. Near the gravel strand is another post 'Men'. Below at the pier top too is all about the strand rules and information is written in Irish. No dance in any house day or night, no one out later than 10.30 and all visitors and all members of the family in at that time for the Holy Rosary. Of course we are keeping the rules as the parish priest wishes us to do so nor neither they would not bless the boats nor sea unless they were promised to do so . . . Such fuss them days from early in the morning till evening and

late in the night and everyone had to be there,
the Island was awful lonely when they went. No
boy or girl here is allowed to walk at night with
any of the visitors nor either in the day time.

VI

Visitors and the Outside World

13.12.31. I am glad you saw Mr Flower or Blaithín we call him *Bláth* that's a flower you know. He is a very nice man, very funny too.

Mary did not come in home yet. A nice boy from Ballyferriter has come in today and I suppose they are looking at him tonight. She forgets me. The night was rather cold and I stayed inside.

22.3.32. A Stranger came in today. He was here twice before, James O'Reilly is his name. He is a barrister. A young man and a nice one too. He don't like dancing atall nor either girls so we are not very glad at his arrival.

Next month anyway we'll be expecting the visitors, or the 'Lá Breághs' as they are usually called around here. You know it comes from the words *lá breágh* means fine day. The visitors used not have only them words and from that they are called 'Lá Breághs'.

18.5.32. There is a youth in Pats Kearney's now. His eldest daughter is home with the last two weeks. I don't know will you see her. The Yank would have plenty of English to give you this time anyway. She is a very nice girl. I like her although it is not every Yank I would like.

There is another stranger here too, a young girl

George Chambers (to whom the letters were written).

and they do have dances in her house every Sunday night, also in Kearney's house since the Yank came.

7.6.32. Mr Flower is here now about a fortnight. His friend from Croydon, a young scholar in Cambridge College, came Sunday last. His name is Kenneth Jackson and he's learning the Irish of course. I talked a lot about you with Mr Flower. I do have great fun with him because he has the Irish, that's why.

16.7.32. The Island is full of visitors at present and we do have dancing every night back at the strand, you know the farthest back strand, well in the green fields near in them.

I met Kenneth Jackson and had a little talk with him but I don't ever go down to the strand with him nor either write his name in the sand, oh no indeed. If George [Chambers]was here we would go down to the strand these lovely evening and write in the sand.

Lots of 'Lá Breághs' or visitors, but none going to Tiaracht Rock yet. I suppose it is a year last Sunday since we were there. The very best day in my life I ever enjoyed. Will a day like it never come again? I wish them days were here again. I would enjoy them lots better.

3.8.32. Another two girls arrived with the postman today. Visitors you know and we are glad. We had a great night in Pats Kearney's last Sunday night, they also have two Dublin girls, young girls I should say. They have their looks yet. The Yank, Pats' daughter, is staying at home this winter too, because there isn't much work in America these days. They are expecting more visitors and they have the uncle's

48

house, who's dead, cleaned up at present, and it is a very nice house too.

1.10.32. Tomorrow Sunday and we are expecting another visitor to Kearney's Hotel. We are all glad of it because the nights are getting long now and we have a dance or something when he comes.

14.10.32. In Pats' Inn now the last two visitors are staying, two young boys and they'll be leaving next Sunday.

Last Tuesday there were only a few letters, none to me, so you could see many other sad faces too turning away from the empty post-bag. Much letters and parcels don't come at present. But it won't be so for Christmas, that's the time you would love the postman to come. I remember not very long ago when I was ten, or maybe twelve, I used never get a letter or no thoughts for a parcel. Mary and myself used be down for the postman every day though we never expected a letter. We don't get them either today but just the same we get letters and parcels sometimes because a few friends has gone to America since and a few visitors that come here once think of us now and then, viz, John Cullen. He visits my aunt's house every year, a middle-aged man never married, nor never will now I am sure. He often sends us a box of sweets, a few hanging pictures or something like that at a time always. Christmas time last year he sent us a melodian. Always every year some nice visitors come and think of some Islander after going away.

My cousin married a Tipperary man, then on their

way home they came to Blaskets. He brought a half
barrel of porter, and whiskey too, and we had a good
dancing night although we girls did not drink anything. Her husband gave her a nice gold watch in
London, he bought if for £2. Well she had everything
she wanted but I don't envy her, I have piece [peace]
and happiness here with my good husband and
father-in-law in this dear Island.

9.7.33. There are many visitors on the Island
already but they are all strangers to us. They all
have my father-in-law's book, *The Islandman*, so
they come to see him.

21.8.33. Well of all years this year was the best,
never before was the Island so full and taken with
visitors. They have all left now nearly and the
Blasket people will have a rest.

Four young boys, teachers, came here with a tent
this year. All the Islanders used be in with them day
and night, and used give them potatoes, fish and
things to eat. Kearneys had lots of visitors this year.
They kept ten and twelve all through.

31.1.34. A stranger reached here a few days ago,
he is still here, he brought in his bicycle and also a
small box of tea. He sells it from house to house, a
young man too. He says he came from Co. Clare.
Never before did anyone come in here selling tea.

24.5.35. A canoe from Dunquin came in yesterday
with two visitors, a young woman and a boy. They
went far on the hill and they told those who were
talking to them that they had spent a couple of
months in London, that they came from New York

and that they'd be sailing away again in the end of the week. The girl also wore breeches or trousers. Haven't they a good time?

17.7.35. I hadn't any visitors this year as my father-in-law isn't feeling well atall, so I have to take care of him his old age now.

13.12.36. Maybe I forgot to tell you before of a family from Birmingham I met with a chance last August. I was just going down to the field to dig some potatoes for dinner, with a spade and a dish in my two hands when I just met them, they were in the wrong way to the White Strand so they wanted [me] to show 'em the right road, they said they hadn't any Irish so I said, 'That's no trouble atall here'. So I was going with them to show them the way and Mary came out of our house and I said that she was my sister, and one of the daughters asked me would I like her to take my photo. I told her I would, and that's the photo I sent you of Mary and myself. After that the wife returned again and sat outside the house painting it. John was in from the sea the same day about the oats and we had tea about twelve o'clock, and I told John as the day was so fine and we were drinking tea, that the woman outside may be thirsty and I would go out and tell [ask]her if she would have a cup of tea. The rest were gone to the White Strand and she was glad to have a cup of milk she said. She do love milk she said and she would come in when I had it ready. I settled a nice cup of milk, a few slices of bread and butter for her and a piece of nice fresh mackrael, she was more than pleased with her lunch altogether — she was not hungry because they brought a lunch with them. We talked during her meal and she had read *Twenty Years A-growing* but did not know anything of *The Islandman,* so we showed her the book, and Tomás too, and she was delighted about meeting us then. She brought in her husband and Martin — the brightest boyeen I ever met — and her two lovely daughters before they went. She was a very lovely wife and she sent Tomás four plugs of tobacco from Killarney. A few weeks ago I received a letter from her and she has *The Islandman* read and was delighted to have seen and met us that day and was very interested in the Island . . .

I am sorry you had not any luck in the sweep. I wish you had, you would send me some of course and I can go to your home and talk and talk until morning about the King, to be sure and about the woman he proposed to at last. John says, he must be insane altogether and if he was only a poor man he would be immediately put into some asylum. Everyone here thinks he isn't himself atall to be drawing such terrible trouble on his people and country and after his noble father King George V. I was crazy to see her photo on the papers but I would not care about her anyway, at any rate, in any way. Would you believe that Edward the Eight is the talk of the Island these days?

22.12.36. I heard about King Edward today, I hope you are not worried about his doings. I am very sorry for him, and I hope his dear Mother and people are not troubled but surely it is a thing even uneducated people here think it a terrible thing that a King to take notice of such a woman.

28.5.37. A crowd of Film Stars has been to Blaskets for a week, eighteen altogether, taking every sort of picture — Blasket has done good through them, money, tobacco and fags for everybody helping them — interesting photos too, canoe racing, five canoes landing in a storm and a man gone out to sea near the canoe and such pictures. Have you seen anything about them on the papers, three Londoners with a filming camera, I am sure you will see these soon, like 'Man of Aran', in a few months time they say. I think this will be called the Islandman.

11.9.37. 'The Islandman', they called that Film is not about my father-in-law — may God rest his soul. I heard it was a man from the University College Dublin, by the way, they are making that film of, you know it means a young man that visited Blasket once and went to college again and then eloped to the Island again and spent his life time there.[The] film then shows you his hard working life here and troubles.

I think Mr Synge was the first visitor that ever visited Blaskets. That time they were not of course as well and able and smart like as they are in the lodging-houses today, as you saw that yourself.

10.11.38. [A letter from John.] I am always on the look out for what Synge wrote about Blasket and I suppose I would not ever read it only for you, thanks ever so much. As far as I understand it I think he wrote exelantly about Blasket. He wrote more to the credit of the place than what he had seen as far as I remember my own childhood days. I and Synge was about the same time I mean a child [John means that he was a child when Synge visited the Blasket]and there is an awful change on Blasket since Synge was here. I would call Synge a clean and splendid writer as for Blasket anyway. All the Blasket people anyhow thought Synge wrote awkwardly about this place and now they do not think so. So to conclude about him I should say for the Final that he was a clean and decent writer.

VII

The Year's Round
(a) Christmas

28.11.31. From this out we'll be whitewashing our houses inside and outside and washing up everything for Christmas. In two weeks time we'll be going to town for groceries for Christmas. Pádraig will go to town next Saturday I think and then only myself will go for Christmas. Last year too it was myself that went. If you were with me what would we do? Ah! I am sure we would do Christmas shopping well.

You tell me all about the nice things you'll have at Christmas. Nice dinners and everything I mean. Will you have any parties in your house? We don't have much things here, of course a small amount of things that we don't use often throughout the year. A sheep is killed in almost every house Christmas Eve here. We do have the walls I mean the top and around the windows decorated with ivy (we don't have holly) and posies we make ourselves.

7.1.32. About my Christmas Day, there is not much to tell about it atall here. The day was not fine atall and no one went to Mass. We went from house to house all around the village and here they have a custom of giving people a half glass of whiskey or half glass of wine at Christmas time; we had great fun drinking it and letting on that we were drunk then singing and everything. After dinner we went to the strand like every Sunday, playing a ball; of course it is the boys that have it, but we do kick it when we get the chance. The boys from the top of the village and the boys from the lower village that play. We enjoy it every Sunday evening now because they are fine. Of course we'll go to Mass every fine Sunday from this out, with God's help.

29.12.35. The weather is very fine here with a fortnight or more, and all Islanders went to Dingle for Christmas groceries. One person from all the house did go as it is an old custom. One who does not go all the year round, do go certainly this time . . . John also did go to Dingle and we are having a very happy Christmas thank God for it. The two men that was with him in town came here Christmas night because they brought a few gallons of stout between 'em and when they had a few pints taken they were singing nicely some old Irish songs which I enjoyed very much. We had tea then about twelve o'clock and indeed none of us weren't very hungry but that is also another old custom at Christmas to have tea late in the night before going to bed whether you feel hungry or not.

Christmas Day was very calm this year and seven or eight canoes were at Mass. They are very glad to be able to attend Mass this time of the year.

25.12.40. All Islanders were out for nine o'clock Mass this morning, some were out for seven o'clock for fear of being late, and they were in for Dinner at one o'clock certainly. All the old and married folk came home but nine or ten of the younger boys stayed out to join the Wren tomorrow, my brother Seán is with them and he brought the violin, also a few girls stayed outside to join in the fun and hall dancing tomorrow night. So its great fun to the young and airy these few days and follow the *Island Wren* from village to village. They were there last year and everyone was generous to them and everyone also enjoys their players' violin playing which is very rare around the country, then when our Island contains only these old couples, the life entirely is gone out of it with the Wren. After tomorrow with God's help the Island will be back to normal when they'll return and will be telling us of their adventures and of those which welcomed them most.

(b) Other Festivals

29.10.31. November's night will be the next night for fun here. We don't have very much of it indeed unless a bit of a dance. We also have other plans a spell of the night. Roasting beans in the fire, two together at a time and we imagine them two beans to be a boy and a girl. After taking them from the fire we throw them into a cupful of water and if they come near each other, ha há dé, that is a good sign you know yourself and if they don't it doesn't matter which, we'll be laughing at the two if they are in the house. Will they be doing anything like that in London's fair city? I am sure not. Oíche Shamhna or Halloween we hadn't much fun because it was a bad night and everybody stayed at home, but as I told you before about the beans. You would use the beans and not having the people present atall, I mean the people you want to make fun of. You can tell 'em in the morning how they got on in the cup. Also we had a big apple hung down from the loft and one person at a time with hands down at your side, trying to take a bite off it. What a pity they hadn't anything like that in London. If I were there I would do something funny.

7.1.32. Shrove we have at present, people thinking of getting married. I don't think anyone here is.

1.2.32. St Bridget's Day here today and the children were out early in the morning before the school opened. Every two boys and two girls together with a small dolls by some of them and others having a big doll which we call here *Brídeog* which means 'Young Bridget'. They get sugar and eggs and pennies. Something in every house.

I often went around the village myself with it but I don't now. In Irish there is a very nice poem or few lines about St Bridget's Day out. I'll try to give you its meaning in English like this:

> It's the first day of February
> From St Bridget's Day on
> The Sun gets very hot
> The sheep soon lambs
> And the cold day is getting longer.

The girls that does go out with young Bridgets, no boy does. Two girls together, one holding the Bridget and the other an old bag or paper for the collection.

5.3.32. St Patrick's Day is very near. Will ye have any band in London? We'll have some old tin here, beating it with something and going around the village in the night you know.

22.3.32. Good Friday will be next Friday and we have a custom here to go to the strand for sea grass and other things that's growing on the rocks. All the women and children go to the strand that day. It is an old custom I think. The women of long ago here used everything that's growing in the strand. They are very healthy too mind you. You of course saw the farthest back strand here. Old men and women say that you should not be in the strand when the sun is gone down entirely. I am sure they used be afraid of fairies.

Next Sunday is Easter Sunday. We'll all go to Mass if the day is fine, I don't know in the world what will you be doing? Do you have any eggs in London? We all here eat three or four eggs Easter Sunday and the men eat more.

16.7.32. St Peter and St Paul. Today is a holiday here. There is a change in the weather. There is wind and rain today and no boat is gone to Mass.

2.11.33. All Saint's Day yesterday. There was nobody at Mass. The day was a stormy but dry. From the field below my house I could see them all on the strand. The boys gathered together and seated on the rocks, the girls back and forth in twos, singing talking and laughing while I had to stay at home looking for things to be done. Their day too will soon come I hope. This day last year I too were on the strand.

I was visiting in my aunt's house. The children too have nice plans, putting four or five saucers on the table, one filled with water, one empty, one filled with clay which meant death for whom would put his hand in it with his eyes closed.

4.3.35. Nobody got married here this Shrove nor with the last twelve years until myself did, the government ought to give me some bounty for being the first for so long a time. What do you think?

VIII

Island Life

18.8.31. Some hard questions in your letter to answer I thought I may get through it somehow today as it is a holiday. They got their provisions from Dunquin most of the time. You see when they are out to Mass every Sunday they bring home their provisions when coming home. Some of them bring as much as will do in the house until next Sunday. Others will bring a month's provision. The people that keep lodgers they of course often send in a note to someone in town to send 'em quantities of teas, sugar, meat, bacon and lots of things. You know they would not get everything they want in Dunquin.

Most of us girls have leave for winter. This is a poor place in the cold winter because I'll tell you why. From this month out their lobster season is ended you know and the people won't earn anything until next April or May for certain. Their little spared money must bring them through all winter now and when they're all big families of course they must do without lots of wanted things sometimes. But God is good and sees everything. Some of them get a help from America of course. They used [to] fish macraels [mackerel]in the past years from this out, but it wouldn't be bought atall these years if it was plentiful.

The children here don't have ever enough of apples or fruit anytime atall. No then poor children. Of course when the old people come from town they sometimes bring them some and that is all.

9.11.31. The schoolhouse was not opened yet and the poor children waiting in the door for Miss O' Shea. Some of them barefooted, others without much woollen clothes while yet others playing around the yard wrapped up nicely without any cold atall. I think they are healthy children here. They do be running from house to house in the evenings no matter how cold it is. Miss O'Shea walks down wrapped up warmly in a fine shawl and when they saw her coming you could see the ones playing in the yard running towards the door and their sods of turf falling to the ground. All the children bring a sod each you know. At playtime they get some bread and jam. They are getting that on all the schools here now.

21.12.31. Now I'll tell you all about my visit to town. My brother Pádraig and a cousin of ours, Seán and myself, went the third time for sheep to the hill about ten o'clock in the morning and by the time we had six sheep in the canoe it was about half-past two in the evening. They were three of us in the canoe, the two boys and myself. The day was very very fine and calm. Three miles then from Blaskets' quay to Dunquin. It was past three before we were in Dunquin. Then you would not imagine what was done. Every two sheep tightened [tied] (in the horns) together. Six we had three each of the boys. We had to face town, to face the road and face poverty that evening. Ten miles then from the top of the cliff in Dunquin to town. We were not a quarter way when it was dark. If you were to see me that night you would pity me of course. The six sheep every two tightened together run up and down in pitches sometimes first you know. But at last they got used to being tightened together and then walked the road nicely together. They got tired you know. Well it was not walking I was atall but running and before we reached Dingle it was about ten o'clock that night. John Moore the butcher bought the sheep. They were not good fat enough — you know this time they don't be very good atall on the hill. They cost a pound each.

Well I was as tired that night and the pains in my legs was awful, I only walked it once before to town. If I would meet you on the street I would hardly know you atall and I suppose it would be the same with you. I went to my lodging house and it was a public house. Mrs Curran's Main St. I took a half glass of wine and also eat supper. Some tea and toast as they often say in novels. I was up early the next morning and attended Mass. I met the other two then. At ten the shops were open. We commenced our shopping, tea and sugar, jam, raison and currants and meat etc. A small amount of every kind you know, three lbs tea and three sts sugar altogether. They are selling groceries in Dunquin you know. I bought a new pair of shoes myself —

brown chocolate colour straps very nice with my dresses and a pair of stockings and a three shilling worth of pinafore to Mary. Boots and trousers were bought by Pádraig and so on.

About half three we hired a motor car, a nice one and we were in Dunquin a bit early. He only charged us 10/6. More of the Islanders were coming to town that day. Men, boys and girls but we were inside home safe and sound at half six o'clock that evening and the sea was very fine also.

7.1.32.   Last night we went into Mitchell's house, you know him (the poor man). He is living alone in the small unfurnished house. His mother living in town, an old age pensioner, supports him. Mary and two more girls and myself walked in to him. His bed is in one corner of the house near the fire. A spring bed and an old mattress without much clothes. A cup and saucer, an old tea pot and a small kettle, also a tin gallon to boil potatoes. He had no flower [flour] last night, no bread only potatoes. He made a big fire but the turf was very wet and he hung the tin on it with some potatoes. He had a job I tell you trying to make a fire of it, which he did in the end and about ten o'clock that time he ate six or seven of the potatoes. The candle was nearly out so we had to come home and leave him alone. We sometimes bring him bread and candles and things because if he were anyway comfortable he'd tell us many stories. He is out of groceries now and the next fine day he'll go out again. He'll go to town to his mother. Poor Mitchell, he has no sense atall. After all he travelled.

3.8.32. Summer is gone away with all its joys and sorrows, some people glad of it, other people sad of it, but that's the way of the world. Autumn has arrived, I hope it will bring peace and happiness to us, soon again winter. Is not it strange? I think it very. A couple of months ago we were so happy thinking of all the strangers and all the fun summer would bring us but now it has passed as quick as I don't know what, and maybe not half being pulled out of it.

14.10.32. Everybody on the Island are very busy at present. Some of the men in the field digging potatoes, others bringing the turf home from the hill. You could see the fields full of people now, men, women and children working hard at the potatoes. They'll be finished with them very soon now with God's Help. They have them stored in now for winter. We had a good potatoes this year too.

17.10.32. Last Sunday wasn't so bad, they were playing football at the farthest back field, you know near the farthest back strand. You see, the boys from the top of the village and the below village were playing, all the old men and women were there. We used call the old women 'nuns on retreat' because they were in one row far back from the crowd, and they would not come nearer, with shawls on their heads. Some with white shawls, others wearing grey and black, while others had brown. The village below won and such laughing and whistling. It was oars they had standing, and when they were coming home then, they put two big white handkerchiefs on

An old woman of the island.

the top of the oars coming over. It was a good joke. Christmas Day they'll try like that again. The boys play football on the strand, while the girls in rows walk back and forth singing together.

21.8.33. They are in from the sea here with the last few days, I mean the fishermen, the sea is rough and wild, so they have another job cutting the corn, also bringing home the turf. The fishermen have a small bottle of holy-water in every canoe and I often saw them when going into the canoe, for to go fishing of course, would make the sign of the Cross. I am sure they have no certain prayers for it only to ask the Lord to bring them back home safe.

1.12.33. Last night was a very bad night, a great storm came. Southerly wind blew very strong. All the Islanders were up all night afraid of the storm. It is the worst wind that does blow here. Everyone today or this morning is talking about last night's storm.

So the sea was rather fine, a canoe went by chance to the mainland – the postman was in it, the others were people who ran short in groceries. They came in safe Thank God. There was a crowd below awaiting, lots of news from outside, people dead and buried since last time, people who were well and healthy the last time they were out. So there will be no one talking about the storm tonight. They'll have more interesting news in the Parliament. There is a house here which they call the 'Parliament'. Only an old widow living in this house and all the middle-aged men gather there in the night from seven to ten o'clock or so. Talking about politics and everything in the world, and when they leave the young folk come there in the end of the night.

1.1.34. On Blaskets from this until I may say April this is when we have winter. The weather is far worse colder in spring and times at all occasions are harder for the Islands. The turf will be getting to its end soon, also the fish that's salted, and the potatoes too where they are big families will be eaten. Anyway the potatoes are very bad here this year, I mean the last time. Of course they buy some in Dunquin for to make the seed for next spring season. Islanders are very hard up during spring season. Things do be plentiful you know until this season.

25.5.34. No turf atall dried on the Island. We have some of last year's yet but very few have it at present because it was put into reeks this time last year and every year nearly. Last year the Islanders had a little money made this time, they had some fishing done, and today they had none atall. Very poor prices for sheep with the last two years, from 12/- to 18/-. A very fat sheep to reach a £1. Before this they used get a £1 at every sheep that was brought to town, so they very very seldom now bring them there atall. Since Christmas now, there was no sheep brought to town nor either did anyone call buying them. Calves too a very low price entirely.

20.1.36. The men here after breakfast go to the hill every day that is dry and bring the cows and donkeys with panniers on them for turf. It is about one o'clock before they are home then as it is the farthest back turf they are now bringing home and a very good turf it is, hard like coal, and very good fire then these long cold nights. They also keep an eye on the cows and when they come home for dinner, people at home then leave at once and go to the cows again and stay with them until they are brought home about six. From this until April and March great care is taken of the cows because they'll be calfing that time. So this is the worst time of the year for Islanders, no milk and no fish by some of the large families, anyway only for the dole I could not think how some people here would ever manage with the last two years because they didn't make any money at lobsters. Anyway I am milking our own cow yet, she keeps it until very late and she won't calf until the end of April.

The men then in the evenings settles up fences of fields for the spring. The women are locked up inside this time and the young girls hasn't much to do until the evening they take a ramble back to the strand in twos with a shawl around them or for sand to the White Strand. They are visiting in other houses at night until late. The boys plays cards and checkers while the girls chats around the fire.

23.2.36. There are plenty wells here amongst the houses and a very good one at the north side, not so very far for the new houses but years ago when very fine summers came and all other wells dried up they were glad to have this well. Anyway I remember myself with other schoolgirls bringing a canteen of water from this well in the evening and a nice walk it is too. There are also wells far back in the hill but below near the cliffs.

13.4.36. Well dear, there are two kinds of seaweed growing on stones in the strands here. One is a dark red kind of seaweed which is called seagrass, which dry in the sun and is eaten by the people out of their hands as a practise going to the hill or strand, but this isn't a meal atall, it tastes salted. But there is another kind which we call in Irish *sladdie*, I don't know its name in English, which made a very good drink here in olden times, meal-bread and fish were eaten with it. An oven of boiling water first, then the *sladdie* was put into it, and a small grain of salt sprinkled on it, a small timber stick stirring it for a couple of hours. Very seldom it is used atall at present.

Well dear, this is a very tiring time on Islanders, and a very fine and dry weather has also brought lots of work, drawing manure with donkeys to the fields. Fifty and sixty loads as we call them a day, and spreading it in the evening, equal on the ridges with a pike or shovel, and as the weather is so dry, you can't keep on the manure all the time, while turf is dry on the hill, Islanders are working very hard from dawn until evening this time of the year, and manuring is very slow for some of us when the fields are too far from the houses. The cows are put in the fields again and not on the hill, too busy to watch 'em all day.

26.9.38. The lobster season is at an end with the

last two weeks which Islanders are lonely after as always, as there is always something to hand when at sea so when weather breaks this time of the year there isn't much chance of settling it again and just throw Islanders out out of their jobs and their support of life. The last trip of the 'Frenchman' always leaves a sad-eyed look on Island fishermen. They are always lonely to part with him they follow him by land until the ship is out of sight waving and cheering. The fine weather goes with him. Also their only means of living, no wonder then they miss him as fishermen do always miss the sea.

IX

The Inevitable End

10.12.38. Just yesterday another Island home was locked up for good, a relative of myself, M Sullivan, he is sick with the last four or five years. His heart was troubling him he went to hospital and will not return, his daughter went out with him to some friends, a very sad sight for Islanders to see and those parting. are also too sorry to part. So it seems that our Island home is going down year after year and no chance of getting up now that is very sure. So never mind everyone has to put up with his own troubles.

27.2.39. Tonight is very fine and the moon is shining bright and I feel a promising of summer in the air and sky. I feel very light hearted about that but such a night in the Island ten years ago when I was just young is very different from this night. There is no stir or sound in this Island tonight, no children laughing or shouting in the moonlight nor later on by this hour when children would be off in their dreams you could hear miles away with the echoes of the strand rows of fair young colleens in four and five in rows after each other singing lovely Irish songs of love and joy and the older folk with their heads out in the open doors gladly listening to them. The Island is just dead I may say but just for old times sake I sang a few verses myself of the old school songs we used have. Pity you were not listening. There was no one but Niamh alone.

24.3.39. You said it was a pity if Niamh was to be an only child. Well I am sure she would not be if her father was earning £3 a week. Children are not for poor people with four or five shillings a week dole money and nothing else. Surely it's a sin to have children and not being able to give them what they want in life, educations and good jobs, if they can't have that it's better for them not to be born. They are spared around the Island already, no one wants them, they are just in the way, with no money. Don't you see my father and mother today the state they are in with the family reared inside in the house with them yet supporting them.

19.11.39. I received your letter about a fortnight ago and was more than glad as always to hear from you. It was the only and one letter that I got from you which I placed on the shelf unopened which will tell you what hard times and experienced time I have got through since my last letter to you. The local nurse from Ballyferriter was attending little Niamh that same day your letter came so I could not touch it until she was ready and gone away again. Niamh was down with the 'mumps' they call them here, outside around the throat they come, a fortnight ago. She was terrible hot the first night and then she was a little better in the morning but worse again in the evening, we gave her medicine but she used [to]vomit it. She became so constipated then that nothing could move her. She was that way for six days and it was God's Holy Will that let the nurse come to her to releife [relieve] her.

My God such days and nights with storm and thunders and lightening. We used [to]leave her in the cradle until midnight and used [to] be oiling her throat and up and down with her in the midst of the storm looking at our child and that we can't do nothing for her to reliefe [relieve] her. That God in His heaven never again give us such a sight to witness. The day was terrible the six days and the sea was far from being fine but God gave them the chance of going in and out with the nurse and saved our child. Oh God was good to us. She is well again thank God and going around the house but of course she must be looked after awhile until she is as strong as she was. If anything happened to take her away from us the light would be out of my world. I would not care to live after her. So God spared us the joy of our life.

19.1.40. It is the wildest spell that came for years also here. Snow and frost. We are not able to do anything but sit around the fire warming ourselves. I play the ball with Niamh around the kitchen fire to keep us warm. A good fire at night then, you would miss a good book some magazines would be fine for the cold spell.

We are getting 5/- P.O. weekly. John says if he has not a plug of tobacco every week it's not worth living and he has that for 2/- then he has to buy us some weeks a crock of jam and that is now 2/-, 2½ lb

Eibhlís and Niamh.

one, white bread and some things for Niamh. We are all right sometimes of course with so small a family, but I don't know how does the larger family manage. You know its not worth while to be living on 5/- a week. If we could get any chance of any old or new house on the country outside and that John could get any job labouring around that would be heaven to us and that is on your mind and I may tell you the truth tis far from joy for us now to be here like the rest.

3.2.40. I suppose you would be surprised to hear the real history and hardship of Islanders these days that every family is quite tired of the wind and rain and would prefer to be in any other place in the world than here. Meat and food and flour are all gone up in prices and they with other hardships of Islands together leave no hope atall for Islanders. Indeed can't you see that the Island is bare with only one child and three at school with no hope or promising of any other but just a face telling you from day to day that this Island will be with none atall but rabbits some fine evening and it is not fit for any other nature, Islanders see nothing before them these days, the children grow up and no good place to go, the children of the Island seven years ago are men and women with their future blanked and black and of course they would not dream of any other change for it is high above their reach. The parents now if life was not so dull would be with the last four or five years holding their son's children on their knees and children talking merry and dancing around their kitchen. Do you think the father and mother who is looking of their family getting old and unhappy lacking the pleasure of life which many people enjoy, could be happy themselves, indeed no.

I was inside with an old widow a few night ago, that grey woman you used [to] see in the middle of the village, always outdoor when you are passing, well she had three lovely rooms in her house, her children are all in America only one son that's a man here, but not in her house. Imagine her sitting in the corner alone thinking and looking at her empty house [in] which her grandchildren should be playing and she know that she will never see her dear ones again. Do you think how her heart is, she told me she sometimes don't know where is she atall or what's going to happen her and she sleeps very very little. Then when storms come she is frightened to death that the fairly big house will fall down on her. Do you think she minds what happens her or which country that will win this war. She could not either understand which would be the best for her, either she don't care. Nothing will take her out of this place now but her coffin and alas she is buried alive already with rather a long time.

10.6.40. You may be sure that the Island is very much affected by the black cloud, I should say it is terrible this summer season and it is no happiness atall. Now when the Island should be in bloom as with many years there is no life atall in it. How would be? Only one canoe came out fishing. There is a blight on lobster fishing the season with no hope of the rescurer, the poor man, maybe he is dead one of these fine days. Indeed I may tell you that shillings are far and scarce at present, when young and old used have enough, even the married men were deprived of the 'dole' this week. What do you think of that? But God is good and may open some gate for hope with His Holy Will. There is peace and want, I thank God it's not war amongst plenty as it is where it is. Flour now in Dunquin, ½ sack 30/- tobacco 2/- per plug, 2 lbs butter 3/-.

29.6.40. Only the one visitor has come to the Island yet, it's a hopeless, fruitless year, everyone thinks so, even the weather is miserable. Fishermen are doomed by sky and sea so far, only two canoes are out and a terrible storm has come to blight every growth in their bloom. It's in the air that every living thing or person must suffer more or less. It's awful to live these days. I hope you are safe from the air raids and killing and all the troubles there. There is peace and God's blessing on this Island so far, thank God.

10.8.40. Another house has been closed on the Island lately. She was an old woman – the Kearneys' mother – and she went out to her daughters she had an only son in the house and he himself used leave the Island every winter and stay in the same house his mother stays now. So picture our Island home sinking from day to day.

25.12.40. Two weeks ago Patrick Daly, Senior, E Dunleavy, a Guiheen boy and my own brother Pádraig went to Inishvickilane to stay for the night killing rabbits and such a storm came they stayed a week there. We were all afraid because they had not much flour nor tea nor groceries, but they had plenty potatoes and eat flour only once a day — that was breakfast time. They killed plenty rabbits and eat them with the potatoes twice a day they hadn't any pinch of salt either. The two older were very disgusted with the storm and high wind, they slept together in their clothes (as there is not any beds there at present) near a very large fire with their oil coats thrown down on them. So one of the men said he was so deaf from the wind that he could not stand it any other day and if it wasn't calm tomorrow to dig him a big hole in the ground opposite the house so that he would go down there and would have a rest from the wind. It was terrible strong too about four days and nights and the seas were so high going up on the mountain. How would you like to be there like that?

6.2.41. 'The last night came to an end and the cocks began to crow' so did the school of the Island a fortnight next Monday I think it was 27th Jan. A notice came to the teacher to close the school at once from the Parish Priest so next day she [the schoolmistress] bid the Islanders adieu after about seven easy years teaching and left the three poor scholars to run wild with the rabbits, which is their delight indeed. I hear they will be sent out to some outside school and that the Government will pay for their board. She was expecting another year anyway from them this teacher as they were her own scholars.

22.3.41. You have asked me a question in your last letter about the girls and their husbands. You see that them girls married outside, love the Island still and love the people they left there but could not find enough courage to marry there as married troubles are great ones and they could not face them inside these days with no old women helpers or any women, you know as the people are reducing so is their courage going . . .

25.11.41. There will not be any candles this year, I have two since last year which will do Christmas night and the night after. There isn't any paraffin oil with the last two months and the old custom which we call *slige* that is the cover of a box of shoe polish with wick covered with seal or fish oil that is the small light, on everybody's table these long nights. We don't complain of it, and a good turf fire burning and nobody is hungry so far thank God for that. Islanders feel happy amidst hard times until anybody is sick this time of the year always.

23.2.42. We have determined at last to leave this lovely Island, I know you will be very sad to hear it, but things are not as they should be and times are changed and expecially for us here with a child at school age and no school and people saying and telling us the child must go to school very soon. They may take her away somewhere when they think of it you would know, so we thought it best to go out somewhere ourselves and try and have at least one joy out of this hard life, to live with our child. So the next time you will come to this Island there will not be no Eibhlís but the ruins of the house, only the walls as we are taking out the head [roof] of the house there near Ballydavid as Seán's friends are living there on fishing. He will go out fishing there with them. You may be sure I'll miss the calm air or our dear Island and the beautiful White Strand. You know people interested in Eibhlís and the Island would not do. Visitors coming in and going out of our house talking and talking and they on their holidays and they at home having comfortable home and no worry during winter or summer, would never believe the misfortune on this Island no school nor comfort, no road to success, no fishing, not five hundred of mackeral was caught when last summer it cost £3 a hundred, no lobsters last summer, very very scarce, hard times, everything so dear and so far away. Surely people could not live on air and sunshine. No not at all. There are two more families leaving also with us. I can't really say what time we are going out, April or May. I will know in my next letter.

I was very troubled when this commenced but when I am understanding and looking at it from other sides I am getting all right again, for instance girls who grew up with me and went to America years ago and made their home there, never saw their parents since nor the Island, surely I have shared many I may say happy years there; whatever happens on this Island I have one gifted thing to tell you of it I was always happy there. I was happy among sorrows on this Island. I think I will not be interesting in life atall from this on when I am gone out on the Mainland. I will be very sad to leave my parents.

4.4.42. Yesterday Good Friday Niamh and I visited the Gravel Strand as it is an old custom here to bring home something to eat from this strand this holy day, also John was there picking limpets or in Irish *Báirneach*. He had a ½ gallon tin full. I counted thirty people there, men almost all only five or six girls. The men were going out to the very end out cutting seaweed and carrying in small amount roped in through the large stones. Indeed it was a great task, and taking them up to the field where the ass can come for it. Before it was spread on the fields ready in the late cold and raining evening, you may be sure they had done a good day's work. They haven't any good hopes of good potatoes this year without guano which is very very scarce, they will be very very wet but anyway they are making the best of what they have like always and hope God to help them for the rest. You may be sure that poor Islanders work for their meals and to tell the truth has a very poor meal after the day and is too far from some good food or a good drink to take after their hardworking day. They were all very wet in the strand that day.

14.5.42. I will try and give you a full view from the air on our Island at present. We had a most glorious weather with the last three weeks and as always Islanders think they are just on the mainland while it lasts moreover these days, then you go out and buy ½ lb coffee and no sugar is there, no soap, no tea, no tobacco and the worst of all no flour nor bread nor biscuits nor paraffin oil for light nor a candle. Yesterday the day being beautifully calm two Islanders went to Dunquin and walked it all the way into town. One of these was the Queen's son Mike the Poet and the other was Keane who is seventy years of age and they walked and tramped it all the way from town more late in the evening, this old man carrying three stones of flour on his back. You may understand these hardships on Island life and you may be sure that there is a certain strain of body and mind and able to age a good young man of strength and energy. And to make matters worse these men could not light their pipes after their hard day's ordeal after their resting at home late in the evening as they did not get a pipe of tobacco in town. It was the same with two younger boys before this and their families at home were gone to bed before them without eating any bread all day save a few old potatoes which is not worth much from now on unless you have saved the bigger ones and put them apart, but Thank God we have them for indeed many the meals they make and they are too glad to have them. I am afraid they won't go far now by some of them as they are making two good meals of them during winter and then [where]there is a cow and a calf and also an ass asking for some potatoes are easily exhausted.

6.11.42. Niamh was attending school for a month and it closed then as some fever broke out around.

She is more happy here among a class of her own than in the Island, she was missing the joy of a group of children laughing and shouting. She always likes to be writing and having a book pretending to be reading and singing. When she is asked would she prefer this place to the Island, she alway says 'I would rather being in the Island'. Its 9.30 and Niamh is thinking of going to bed and before Rosary is said and the fire is settled up and the table for John some bread and butter and some milk in the saucepan for to heat for him. We have a better chance here of getting our rations than on the Island, my God things are difficult enough to get on the mainland and you may be sure that living on Islands is no joke atall these days. To tell you the truth I am glad (in spite of being lonely after them) of being out in the cold and dreary nights of winter.

8.1.43. The oldest person on the Island died in the middle of Christmas some days ago; his age was ninety-six. His name was John Kearney, a next door neighbour of us in there. He was blind with the last eight or nine years and he had a miserable life there in latter years for his son married in his house died four years ago and his wife the year before. His own wife died suddenly in his best house and everything was going from bad to worse for him, no doubt he was strong and healthy, he can say it. May he rest in peace, Amen. He said there lately if all went well as he would like them to go on he would live more than a hundred but unless he was all iron he had to break down. Only one canoe was in the funeral, that brought out the corpse, the day was not well and they were shocked by the bad weather and outside the landing place in Dunquin, the quay nearly all went by the storm so it's all a wreck there unless in a very calm weather. So everyone tells us we are lucky to have come out this year. I am glad we are also for Niamh's sake and by God when the young people are leaving, sure its no place atall then. You come out to Dunquin then you will not get what you like to get, then after a hard day's toil going rowing out and in again you will come home without that thing you badly want. Of course its changing from bad to worse from day to day.

10.2.43. Well dear friend we are in the beginning of the New Year and thank God we are all well and happy so far and have enough to eat and drink as always. I think we are very lucky to have been out this winter for it is the severest winter that came with ages and even yet it is bad and very bad and such rain and snow nearly every day. In the bad weather I don't miss my lovely Island so much but in the warm weather of course I think of the beautiful scenery of my Island which I did not admire so much until now. Of course with God's help I will see them all again some day during the summer season, how I'd love to see my parents once again and all my friends and throw myself once more on the White Strand.

8.12.45. Please God I will visit my Island home early in the New Year if I get any chance atall and see the old parents and friends. Niamh showed me a

book a few nights ago and a photograph of the old
house in the Island in it, I was nearly crying when I
saw it, though sands of memories were running
through my mind of how I used see the old pictures
of the sea so calm and the seagulls crying and the
canoes coming in from the mainland and the White
Strand, white with white sand, how crowds of us
after school used [to] play together on it like one
family, so scattered now and not even one child on
this lonely white sands. A great pity. What do you
think?

2.12.51. To tell you the truth about Niamh my
plans for her is to cross the ocean when the time will
come and that is, that she will be strong and healthy
enough to do so. To go over to America the country
of the poor and for the poor, for the parents here in
Ireland would be naked out only for their children
go over in time, to send money to pay for their debts
and send every stitch of clothes for bedding, curtains
and human use. Everything from America.

30.12.51. How quickly the years gallop away as
you say. I was sitting here by the fireside a few
nights ago and I was looking on the old clock which
is in a glass-case, the one we had in the Island and
it's the same glass-face that's on it, I was thinking of
how often Tomás — The Islandman — looked on the
same clock nobody could count, and a snap of
yourself was inside in a corner of the clock. Well I
had so many things running through my mind, some
gay and many sad memories too, I was thinking that
you often too made me happy since I married al-

86

ways sending parcels and things and thank God said I, I have him again this Christmas behind me and Niamh will be with me a few more Christmases but then I am sure I will not be happy any more then. The old folk of the Island will be scattering to their graves and no more Island holidays then, and such and such were coming before my eyes near the fire. I think more and more of my Island home Christmas Eve than any other time and a terrible storm has just passed and Seán (my brother) will not come out atall this year and I missed [him] very much. Do you ever have such dreams? You do not have time to yourself to do so I suppose.

THE MAN FROM CAPE CLEAR
Conchur O Siochain
Translated by Riobard P. Breatnach

Conchur O Siochain lived all his days on Cape Clear, the southern outpost of an old and deep-rooted civilisation. He lived as a farmer and as a fisherman and his story portrays the life of the island, (Fastnet Rock's nearest neighbour). He was a gifted man in many ways and developed great skills as a storyteller, a folklorist and a craftsman. The book is a collection of memories and musings, topography and tales, descriptions of old ways and crafts, and contains a fund of seafaring yarns and lore.

MALACHI HORAN REMEMBERS
Dr. G. Little

Malachi Horan Remembers is real and stirring history caught from living lips, just in time to save a hundred quaint, beautiful precious things from oblivion. The book is a revelation. It describes authentically a purely Irish, robust, picturesque life, like that of unspoilt Donegal, Connacht or Kerry — thriving in the lifetime of the teller, on the hills that can be seen from Dublin's streets. Hedge schools, wooden ploughs drawn by bullock teams, fairy lore, quaint folktales, unique relics of Leinster Irish, road tolls — all are described by one who knew them. County Dublin, we see here, is truly an Irish-Ireland too.

'This is a darling book. The general reader will devour it for sheer delight. The folklorist already has pronounced it a treasure.'

THE TAILOR AND ANSTY
Eric Cross

The Tailor and Ansty is the day-book of the Tailor and Ansty's fireside talk. Their fireside was a place of call for a whole host of people, from near and far. The talk ranged over many aspects of Irish peasant life and character. There are stories of the marriage customs; of the coroner's inquest; of funeral orgies; of the Tailor's travels — which went no further than Scotland in fact but extended to America in imagination.